Take Charge! Of Your Personal Finances

Kudzai M. Mubaiwa

An IS Motivational Series Book

Published by IS Publishing House

Copyright © 2012 by InvestorSaint
(Private) Limited

All rights reserved.

www.investor.co.zw

God blessed them:
"Prosper! Reproduce! Fill Earth!
TAKE CHARGE!

Genesis 1:28 Message Bible

ISBN: 1495251772
ISBN-13: 978-1495251771

DEDICATION

To My Parents: Mr Tennyson Maraire – for building confidence in me to achieve all things money & Mrs Margaret Maraire – my first personal banker, financier and joint venture partner

Contents

DEDICATION iii

Introduction – A Call To Action! i

Chapter 1 - I Could Use A Bit More Cash 1

Chapter 2 - Choose Freedom! 5

Chapter 3 - Bring Back The Piggy Bank! 8

Chapter 4 - Increase Your Net Worth! 12

Conclusion - Leave A Legacy! 16

ABOUT THE AUTHOR 18

About Investor Saint (Private) Limited 19

Books In The Motivational Series 20

INTRODUCTION – A CALL TO ACTION!

This is an urgent call to action, by an entrepreneurial warrior. The stakes are high for you and your posterity! How you manage your money today will impact not only you, but your children and children's children.

At the time of print it has been over three years since the multicurrency regime. Without doubt the use of the United States dollar, South African rand and Botswana pula brought some stability. Whatever we held of Zimbabwe dollar culminated to zero value, and we are building again. With some sense of economic sanity restored, we have steadily though slowly regained our confidence to transact more (by both volume and value), as individuals, families, institutions, corporates and as a nation.

I have **unfortunate** news though – that all you/we have done up to now is (again) under threat - and it's not by GNU politics or even sanctions; but by YOU!
Fact is, how you choose to behave financially is of great consequence - first to you, and second to the generations that come after you.

You and I will explore this in the subsequent pages and see the real threat(s) to your present and future prosperity, as well as the opportunity available to escape poverty and grow wealth for your own benefit, your family, community, institution/corporate and ultimately, your nation!

I believe I have written in a simple manner, which anyone can understand. You will realize that the option of financial freedom is in your hands, and I urge you, when you choose, to CHOOSE FREEDOM!

Freedom is available for those who will **take charge**.

Unto your wealth,
K.M.Mubaiwa.
Harare, Zimbabwe
March, 2012.

CHAPTER 1 - I COULD USE A BIT MORE CASH…

Could you use a bit more cash? I know - so could I! It seems no one can ever have enough money. In fact, if you are honest from where you stand/ or sit (!) you can easily come up with some figure which would probably 'solve' all your present financial woes. Before you dream up 'what could be', how about we audit 'what is'.

So you have 'X' dollars at your disposal every month, from your employer/business/well-wisher.

How about a few tough questions?

Do you make the best use of that money? As in rational best use, ensuring that you cover all the basic essentials for life; within the present limits?

Do you actually have a budget or is your idea of budgeting pulling whatever you need out of your pocket or purse until it's all gone?

If you do have the discipline of writing some kind of financial plan/budget every month – do you **really** stick to it? Or do you just say what the heck and throw it out the window, along with caution to the wind?

As someone put it - do you always find yourself with more <u>month</u> leftover than money?

Are you living on your earned cash or off 'other people's money' [OPM] in an unhealthy way?

Are you always needing a soft loan to get you to the next opportunity to get rich (a.k.a payday!) and your whole life collapses if the pay date is moved by a single day? Funny, but in a sad way!

So what are the things that feature on your budget? What are the spending patterns or trends?
What are the vices and habits funded off it?
Do you have any room to maneuver in the event of some unforeseen (and there always will be) cash-needing event.

Are you still standing on firm ground?
What is your present (economic) net worth?

That is the resulting figure on netting off what you own and what you owe. (Put aside all the intellectual property in your head!) It's pretty sobering to often take stock in that direction. It may shock you to discover that you have absolutely no capacity to absorb all your dues if the rug were pulled (literally!) under your feet today.

How are you funding your present lifestyle?
Is it by consumer debt?
Can you afford it?
I'm not talking of buying power here but the effects and demands thereof!

Isn't it just amazing how if you weren't stuck in all those monthly payments then even your **present remuneration** would be sufficient to allow living a reasonable life?

The cold, hard truth is many of us do not leave within our means. We live a standard that isn't necessarily in line with what we earn, yield or receive.
I have no issues with comfortable living, but I'm not going to stock up on all sorts of nice things at the cost of a debt burden. Worse still I won't have the 'private pressure' of debt for the sake of the 'public pleasure' of keeping up with the Jones, or in our Zim case the Makonis, Ndlovus or whoever else I come into contact with. For all we know we

may **all** be putting up a show! And we might never know it!

I have thus learnt to say **no**! I militate against consumer debt; I flee it in its every form and fancy name – account, arrear, line of credit, pre-purchase, accrual...etc. I call it by its real name – **DEBT**. Then I refuse it to its face (or the unfortunate agents face!).

Recently I shocked two sales agents in a local clothing store when I refused to buy a $12 shirt on account. Come on people, do you really need 3 or 6 months to pay for a shirt that might be fading by the time you complete payments? The pain of parting with your cash is better felt that one time than have number of (bullet) payments (no wonder they call them that, they really are a pain!)

And so effectively have some pain every month. Add that little pain to a number of other 'jabs' from all over and you have yourself a real problem every month when the money hardly sits in your hand as it flows to its more astute owners (not you!).

I do agree it (seems to) makes great deal of sense at the point of purchase, but can someone testify of the experience at the point of **payment** please! When sometimes you can't even recall what exactly you bought by the way...?!

So if you do have the discipline to pay monthly, can you not convert the same high virtue to putting something away **until** you have enough to purchase cash?! There will always be a top, shoe, bag, piece of technology that looks like it has your name or is speaking, no calling to you.

Want to dare? Try catching up with mobile phone models just this year alone, and let's talk about it end of year. I suggest you ignore that voice for once and check if you die!

For goodness sake, stop the bleeding! So, tell us now - **who really is in charge of your finances?**

Is payday a non-event?

We can remedy that. Stop the bleeding. Be aware that when you get rid of payments you have the largest wealth-building tool in your life available to you – your present income. When all the money comes in and quickly goes out, there's nothing to invest or save or buy nice things with. But it's easy to do all these things when you don't have any payments. And it's more satisfying to reward yourself with that nice item when you have saved for it.

Someone forgot to ring the bell when we crossed over to multiple currencies. You don't **have** to buy it today in case in goes up tomorrow, in fact, as time passes and competition increases you are likely setting yourself up to benefit from better prices OR the powerful negotiating power that comes with holding cash in your hand! Cease borrowing from your future today!

Begin to fill up the hole (or crater), starting with the most expensive one. Negotiate a payment plan if you must to freeze the dues where they stand and show strong commitment by living up the payment plan, and even speeding up payments where possible. It's worth it for your freedom!

Oh, they didn't tell you – consumer debt is the modern day form of slavery – and it's so sophisticated, your 'master' makes you think you are the one in charge when you are not.

They hide the chains and call it 'interest-free'. They say you can take your time and pay at ease – try missing a payment then you'll see who's got the power!

They'll even increase your 'buying power' (read borrowing power here) for good behaviour – giving you a longer chain! Modern day slave is what you are, dressed in a half-paid-for designer suit, spending money before you earn it such that at month-end the budget is already determined by creditors. Who did you say was in charge of your finances again? Take Charge!

CHAPTER 2 - CHOOSE FREEDOM!

Are you living within <u>your</u> means? If not, then whose means are you living off?! I have observed, learnt and appreciated that simplicity is key – and little changes / adjustments to your life can add up to much.

When I started working I spent inordinate amounts of money on candy. The chocolate I favoured cost about a dollar, and I had at least one or two a day. If I had put that away since then till now, never mind the compounding interest effect, by now I could be enjoying that all expenses paid trip to New York City!

Take a long, hard look at your life and you will see there are places you can tweak. Do you and your spouse critically need two cars every day to work? Must you have full DSTV to be entertained (especially if you only watch selected programs during the weekend - never mind during the week)? Aren't you better off renting/buying the movie when you need it?

Do you need the full year gym membership when you live in a neighbourhood where you can make do with an evening jog that can be coupled with me-time or quality time with the significant other? Do you need a suit in every colour? #think UTILITY#

Remember the old time Sunday best? When we were kids, all of us at Sunday school could identify each other a mile off because we almost always wore the same thing to church every Sunday. We were not lacking, we were simple! Now, it's another thing. I once overheard a mum fighting with a 3 year old at Avondale flea market who wanted a certain type of ....wait for it....hipsters. Hipsters! At age three! (You see why we really have to take charge, not just at economic level but a whole lot of other socio-moral things!)

What we need to do more often is to choose to walk free. Free from the concerns of owing, and free to choose our destinies rather than have them cut out for us on the basis of the strength or weakness of our economies.

The man/woman who has strengthened his/her economy is free to choose, what to eat and wear, where to stay, when to go. All of us desire that freedom, yet we do not do enough to attain it and thereafter maintain it.

I am in a militant mode and mood against anything that would threaten that freedom in my life. I have extended it to my business. I am so serious about it; it has cost me some relationships. There has to be some collateral damage in every revolution. I have set it in my mind that I want to be able to afford it. I am working from where I am, with what is in my hand to achieve it.

Sell something if you must for the sake of a good night's sleep and a good name! I had this conversation with a friend some weeks back. I applaud her and her husband for their commitment to choosing freedom. They backed it with action - sold car their second to clear debts. Did they live happily ever after? Nop, not in this story: they lived happily for some time. Then they got carried away and accumulated more debt.

They got back into a quagmire, made a tough decision to sell a bit of real estate to unlock value, bought something more affordable and a smaller economic vehicle, plus cleared all outstanding amounts. Now they are building themselves up. Greatly humbled but are free. Don't you want to be free too? There are actions you can take.

First, **decide it**. This a tough one, not for the faint–hearted because your decision will be tested – by shopping mates, by goods in shops, by close relatives who will need favours and those that claim to use debt as a leverage – which it can be – but have been unsuccessful in harnessing it themselves!

It's possible to live within one's means and do more. Of course it is. One of my greatest marvels has been how teachers and other noble civil servants have been able to just survive let alone marry traditionally and wed! All this off a salary which is public knowledge! So there you are- you won't die.

You do need the strong resolve though that you want to move from 'poverty and want' to 'prosperity and have'.

That strong decision will need to be followed by **remedial action**. That's the surest demonstration of conviction. Track your own leakages and plug them. Some will be okay if you nip them in the bud but a great deal will require to be literally uprooted from the roots in the ground!

It won't be a once-off transaction; you will need to **continually** act militantly against consumer debt as it confronts you. You will need to recognize it and call it by name so that you can vigorously reject its' advances. You will need to re-determine the boundaries and requirements for your new life. Some of them will be painful and most of them uncomfortable. But then again, such is choosing freedom!

Choose freedom and so take charge!

CHAPTER 3 - BRING BACK THE PIGGY BANK!

How much do you put away for a rainy day or a holi-day? For that high tech gadget you so want? For postgraduate education (it's real expensive!)...or...for your own pension! (Company takes care of that I hear you say – laughable at least!). A local paper recently was showing the latest rates and pay-outs on social security, went up some 100% and yet remained peanuts. Why leave your fate to another – when you can take full charge? Try saving, it still works!

I did the math. I left a job recently and calculated what I would likely receive in pensions, at least for the dollarization period. Allow me to repeat myself – the amount is laughable at the very least. With twenty dollars stashed monthly under the pillow each month of the same time period, I would still have been relatively better off doing it myself – even taking account of inflation! Bring back the savings culture I say! Restore the piggy bank. Beware of its extinction.

Teach it to your children - savings is a discipline not a luxury. In fact it's premised on spending – deferred spending. I did the math – putting away just $50 every month or $150 a quarter will mean my presently 2 year old boy can be buying a reasonable car of his choice by the time he is driving at 16! (And so reduce the squabbles over the family car!)

If we are to adopt the American dollar then lets at least also adopt the **positive** behaviours of its' people. The typical American saves. A notable portion of present income is put away in investments – for unfortunate incidents, holidays, college fees and inheritance. Many of us African folk and more so Zimbabwean folk save nothing, preferring to live the more adrenalin filled life of encountering enormous pressure suddenly when things are due. An unfortunate incident can set you back horribly, if you are unprepared. You will be surprised how you can have a lovely holiday (**not** going to the rurals!) when you have been merely setting aside a little each month.

It won't be forfeited to the state; it will abound to your account. That's called delayed gratification – and it's within everyone's capacity regardless of how much (little!) they earn.

Delayed gratification is exactly the principle at work when you are presented with a plate of sadza, green vegetables and stewed beef. You attack the sadza, veggies and soup with vigour, and interact with them more than the meat which many of us 'save' to eat last. For the joy that is set before us we fill ourselves with the less tasty portion of the meal, for we hope that at the end we shall close it off with the superior taste and texture of meat in the mouth! So there you go: you have done it before – yes you can! ten per cent of your income would be ideal for savings, as and when you receive it. However, with the knowledge of incomes that are still growing and in many instances well below the poverty datum line, for the sake of the discipline of saving it can be a lower percentage, say 5% OR a fixed amount periodically.

It's the discipline and the consistency that is required. Sadly, much of that is lacking in the typical Zimbo. Dare to defy that norm!

There are a number of options available to save, ranging from unit trusts to savings account right through to holding gold or land. Whatever correct thing it may be you can start doing today in that direction – please do! Shop around for the best deal in such transactions, ask friends, ask even the service providers what they deem are their unique selling points. Go for the best mix of return and solid company credentials.

Inculcate a savings culture in your children. I salute my mother for this one. We were fortunate to grow up with the opportunity to relate with our grandparents – and back in the day it was almost certain that on their departure from visiting our house, we would get monetary gifts. 'Sadly' for us, we would only handle that money at the point of receiving it. Mum, our first personal banker; would almost immediately step in and offer to 'keep it for us'. (I think she used some as bridging finance!)

If we were lucky enough to be let go with the money in hand, she would pointedly remind us of the POSB books we each had, in our own names.

The practice of depositing money into the bank was such a pain, but at the same time I will never forget the awesome feeling I had when years later I used the same book to withdraw some money from the local post office and purchase goodies while I was at junior high school at a mission school – we were always hungry!

The pain became the pleasure and even the pride later of being the only one in my stream to have an ATM card from Barclays when I was in form 3. In my late teens I convinced my mother to participate in the listing of Fidelity – the insurance company and I put in something of my own. We exited a little time later with a modest gain by Zim standards of a 60% gain – and I can recall the exact items of clothing I purchased from the profit on my investment.

Starting young helped me to be confident concerning financial matters and it is my intention to ensure all of my children, and really all people I can come into contact with, would embrace the value of savings – putting away something now for the future.

Consumerism is one of saving's greatest enemies. The culture of must-have-now and must-buy-now is certainly intoxicating. However, you and I must look further ahead, far enough ahead to see why we must have the discipline of resisting the urge to 'spend all we got – in case tomorrow we die!'

Not all your savings are to benefit you. Some are for your children's sake – if you died today – would they have something to live on? Would you spouse curse or bless your very grave once they see how little (much) you leave them as an inheritance? One who is really in charge of their finances has the ability to save something, no matter how little, towards a specific goal. Name it (the earmarked money) before you save for it so that you can honestly check your own progress objectively.

If the goal is a new laptop, you can find the indicative cost and target to have the say $1,000 available in 5 months. Hence you need to save

$200 each month till the 5th one. That's a clear goal.

The "saved-for–item" must be clearly visible to all, so that it is protected from all 'emergencies' that arise – sickness or death. Those must have their own fund. Once you begin to enjoy the fruit of past and targeted toils, you will find that saving becomes much easier. Let go of some takeaway junk food often patronized by young couples and bachelors - channel that amount towards savings if you see your budget is inflexible and can't free anything to save. Make the decision and open a fixed deposit or unit trust account somewhere. Authorize them to directly debit you.

Put away something, and by so doing, take charge!

CHAPTER 4 - INCREASE YOUR NET WORTH!

How would you like to choose your lifestyle? It's not impossible. You only need to **make enough** to afford/ pay for the next level, where you eat what you want, wear what you want, live where you want (including under water!) and travel where and how you want. You have the leeway to what you want to and not just what you have to!

The answer lies in growing your wealth. There are numerous ways to do that and these include sweating your present assets, increasing your knowledge, increasing your streams of income. We will look at these one by one.

You can grow wealth by sweating your present assets. It is said the typical human being uses much less than their God-given capacity. If you are to be frank with yourself, sit down with pen and paper and think up ways to increase income from **just what you have** and where you are. It would be shocking how soon your quality of life could improve.

Of course you may be past that, but do the second, nobler thing, act on it! I totally agree that most successful people are so inclined not because of any marvellous reason other than that they fully exploited the opportunities that crossed their paths! For some it was just one opportunity but they had the ability to grab it as if it was the last one on earth and diligently work it till it translated to revenue.

What are the evident opportunities, the low hanging fruit in your path? What could you do today, **from where you are** that could impact your bottom line with a great big ka-ching-ching?!

If you are employed you might need to just make sure that you put in a little more work so that you can be recognized and be promoted. Or you are already overworked and juggling the work of four – how about asking for a raise? That's exactly what I said, use the Oliver Twist precedence and **ask for more!** Or have you self-developed and have that elusive masters none else has in your department (including, sadly; you immediate manager)?

Ask for greater responsibility and the benefits that come with it. It may not come as what you require or when you require but anything to recognize your quality input is worth it.

If you are unemployed, **great** – the asset you have is time. The only difference between you and someone employed is that you have 'unsold time' – time that is not being exchanged for value. Find ways to derive income from that time, whether it be offering a service or upping your skills in something that will sharpen you in some income-yielding ventures. Some ideas are being pushed by less qualified people than you and you can see evident weakness in their operations, but they remain superior to you because with all your knowledge you are not implementing what you know.

Let's go to the tangibles. You have two cars – one for each of the spouses, yet one or both of them are driven just 20 minutes to work and another 20 back. Spends its' day in the car lot, gossiping with other cars and running up a city council parking bill for lying idle during the most productive hours of the day.

Find it some daily chores, short term hire, or commuting so you get value. Same as home space which can be converted into paid storage space. Or a 9 to 12 closed play group. List what you are doing now and what you can do from where you are and take charge of sweating those opportunities today. Do them unto completion, even if it means doing just one thing at a time till it is completed or at least can stand alone.

What's happening around you today?
What opportunities present themselves to you?
Who do you know who can assist you?

Many Zimbabweans regret ignoring calls to sign up for land during the redistribution exercise – while they were still contemplating pros and cons some had already staked out the land!

Indigenization, that "dirty word" in fact presents a sterling opportunity to participate in increasing the nation's well-being, and thus one's own.

How about positioning yourself?

We often have great ideas, dreams and projects but unless we take ourselves seriously soon and get a move on already with what we have - then I'm afraid we shall be victims of our own complacency, filled with delusions of grandeur yet achieving nothing notable. Do everything required to get the maximum return from all that you own, that in your hand. Take charge today!

<u>You can grow wealth by increasing what you know.</u>
A proverb says: "a wise man will seek after knowledge and wisdom." The truth is to get to the next level you may be required to get more knowledge. It is again said that one can hardly move beyond that which they know. It is critical to invest in yourself, for ignorance is definitely more expensive than knowledge, whichever way. School is great for giving you leverage and also positions you at a superior place to the unschooled. This includes both the formal structure as well as 'street smarts'.

With the proliferation of technology, everything you know little about is a click away! Are you up to speed with the latest trends worldwide, at least in your chosen career path or business line? Do you know the latest innovations? The more you know, the better you can identify and utilize opportunities.

A proverb says success tends to follow the prepared. Are you preparing for that next level? So you want to be a successful farmer or career banker. What do you know about that area? What's the latest book you have read in that wise? When did you last attend a seminar? Who is mentoring you? How can you widen your base, improve on business systems of what you already run?

I noted this as a weakness amongst many entrepreneurs, lacking the capacity to involve themselves in continuous learning while also managing a business. Increasing knowledge not only stimulates the mind but it often is the basis of friendship and associates who will prove extremely valuable over time.

Set yourself up to receive more by investing in quality education, as often as is practicable.

<u>You can grow wealth by having numerous streams of income.</u> Opportunity and education can be converted to a number of streams of income. Your day job is one, but often proceeds from this cover living expenses only. One must have at least four streams of income, from the north, south, east and west, converging on them!

Use the definite salary to seed each venture and/or proceeds from one venture to start up another. They needn't be large businesses in their own rights, but the fact that one makes an additional dollar at least daily is a good place to start. A simple example: A lady, who works a clerical job at a local bank, also sells airtime at work in the high rise building, as well as breakfast muffins; and plaits hair during weekends. One may not immediately get rich, but at least something will sustain them and the lifestyle they choose. Additional streams of income ought to be cash generating, sustainable ventures.

Cash generating means whatsoever the activity is it must make money – otherwise it's a glorified hobby. Sustainable means it can perpetuate, unlike the money 'burning activity' of late 2008 in Zimbabwe; which was more opportunistic. A guy we know who was a 'dealer' then recently sent an SMS to advise he now does photocopying and other such office support. At least he was able to adjust!

Multiple streams of income are not an excuse to be shoddy. Better grow them one at a time if there are constraints and allow each to thrive than have a number of sickly babies.

What can you think of **now** that you can do now to increase your income?

How about starting?

Do it today, and take charge

CONCLUSION - LEAVE A LEGACY!

Take charge today for the sake of those coming after you. Engage in activities that will guarantee future wealth. A proverb says the righteous man leaves an inheritance for his children's children. May I in the same vein suggest that it is unrighteous to leave nothing for your children, and I'm not talking wisdom of words here but this world's good!

We need to get over the old fashioned fear that once your children know what's in line for them they will kill you. You can die anyway, at their hand or otherwise! Position them in such a way that they will have no excuse, for you will have set them up well for the future.

In fact you will set them up so well, even their children will be partakers of your inheritance. I like that! Encourage **them** to do the same. That's how we set generational wealth and prosperity rolling.

Don't delay, start today!
A number of institutions are now offering that opportunity to lay up for your little ones. Thank God it's USD; it can be traced many years from now. Leave a sizeable inheritance **in addition** to growing them well – with a great education, nice toys and opportunity to travel. All these other things I believe are entitlements for children, and **after** you pass on, you still need to leave them hard cash.

Make it conditional if you want but have the decency to leave something. Do it especially because yours didn't and you know how much that could have helped you. Give them leverage, give them the wings then it's up to them to fly or stay grounded.

But while you work on that cute little nest-egg organize yourself financially. For that pattern of financial management is yet another legacy your progeny receives from you. Let them learn from you the positive actions of working hard, dealing in business, increasing streams of income, budgeting, giving, tithing, saving and investing – and not only learn from you what NOT to do!

Give them the opportunity and the pride to say later in life: "My mum and dad used to do this and it was beneficial in this way..." Let good money habits, attitudes and behaviours be engrained from what they observe you do, and witness its' positive outcome. Let the good be so ingrained such that even when other children praise negative financial behaviours they have the confidence and wherewithal to reject it on the basis of what you have trained them, never departing from it even as they grow. That is the challenge that is laid before us in this day friends, to TAKE CHARGE of our personal finances.

I do hope I have **offended** you into desiring better things and doing them!

I have decided it and am walking that path; will you walk with me beginning today? Just one decision – and you can cross over to **taking charge!**

ABOUT THE AUTHOR

Find her on Facebook on her page:
facebook.com/kumubaiwa.author.speaker

Follow her on twitter:
www.twitter.com/kumub

And email her on kudzi@investorsaint.co.zw
or call +263 772 526 543 for speaking engagements.

ABOUT INVESTOR SAINT (PRIVATE) LIMITED

Find us on Facebook on our page:

www.facebook.com/investorsaint

As well as the interactive group:

www.facebook.com/groups/investorzone

www.investor.co.zw
www.investorsaint.co.zw

BOOKS IN THE MOTIVATIONAL SERIES

- Take Charge! Of Your Personal Finances

- Make More! A guide for multiplying streams of income

- Take Charge! Of Your Small Business

- Woman, Take Charge! Purse Talk for the 21st Century Girl

- Man, Take Charge! Wallet Talk for the 21st Century Guy

- Kids, Take Charge! Piggy Bank Lessons for Toddlers, Tweens and Teens!

- Saints, cents and sense : Money matters for the 21st Century Believer

www.ingramcontent.com/pod-product-compliance
Lightning Source LLC
Chambersburg PA
CBHW070734180526
45167CB00004B/1745